Routedge Revivals

The Hero

The Hero (1925) explains tragedy itself, through a close examination of multiple texts, with a particular focus on Shakespeare. It references many critics in this examination, in an attempt to be as comprehensive as possible.

The Hero
A Theory of Tragedy

Albert Beaumont

First published in 1925
by George Routledge & Sons Ltd.

This edition first published in 2025 by Routledge
4 Park Square, Milton Park, Abingdon, Oxon, OX14 4RN

and by Routledge
605 Third Avenue, New York, NY 10017

Routledge is an imprint of the Taylor & Francis Group, an informa business

All rights reserved. No part of this book may be reprinted or reproduced or utilised in any form or by any electronic, mechanical, or other means, now known or hereafter invented, including photocopying and recording, or in any information storage or retrieval system, without permission in writing from the publishers.

Publisher's Note
The publisher has gone to great lengths to ensure the quality of this reprint but points out that some imperfections in the original copies may be apparent.

Disclaimer
The publisher has made every effort to trace copyright holders and welcomes correspondence from those they have been unable to contact.

A Library of Congress record exists under LCCN 25017610

ISBN: 978-1-032-91508-1 (hbk)
ISBN: 978-1-003-56365-5 (ebk)
ISBN: 978-1-032-91510-4 (pbk)

Book DOI 10.4324/9781003563655

THE HERO

THE HERO
A Theory of Tragedy

By
ALBERT BEAUMONT

LONDON
GEORGE ROUTLEDGE & SONS LTD.
NEW YORK: E. P. DUTTON & CO.
1925

Printed in Guernsey by the Star and Gazette Co., Ltd.

AUTHOR'S NOTE

The work which follows explains tragedy itself. The apperception of tragedy, including the catharsis, will be explained in a future work, to be entitled *The Spectator*.

THE HERO

I

THAT popular " solutions " of the tragic problem are attempts to escape a paradox in the sense, at one and the same time, of free action and the domination of law, is best seen in what might be called limiting cases of this problem. " Infinite fate " or " infinite free-will " answers the coroner in effect, though his verdicts on the man whose gun goes off as he cleans it or who kills himself from apparent caprice may be phrased as " Death through misadventure " or " Temporarily insane."

The mass of tragic incident falls, of course, between such limiting cases. But the influence of " fate " or " free-will " on ready answers to its problem is none the less powerful, if less in evidence. The motive of a suicide (for let me keep to the order of my examples) remains doubtful—until, say, a hidden love-affair is discovered. The man has now killed himself " because he was jilted "—as if, when one is jilted, suicide were an imperative and the only imperative.

Yet it may well seem here that " because he was jilted " *does* answer in part the question, " Why did he kill himself ? " A kind of *fore-problem* has been solved, we think, and we pass on to consider why this jiltee in particular committed suicide. A closer inspection, however, would always reveal the *fore-problem* as either a superficial mystery lying outside the term tragic, or one aspect of a deeper and more general problem that had been seized upon and exaggerated.

Irrelevance and a probable insufficiency of data would mar any attempt to instance from life this last statement. But let us turn for a moment to a world where the appearance of tragedy is clarified and arranged for us. Here is a *fore-problem* whose proportions, of three centuries' growth, insist themselves immediately on our observation in " Hamlet's delay to kill Claudius."

II

The view generally accepted with regard to this delay—that some fault in Hamlet's temperament causes a state of irresolution incapacitating him from a speedy revenge —is also the earliest of any importance. Mackenzie[1] in 1780, following Hanmer's[1] criticism, alludes to Hamlet's " doubts and hesitation " and Goethe,[1] like Parsifal " durch Mitleid wissend," saw a frail and a beautiful nature in Hamlet, faced by a monstrous duty and lacking the strength of will for its performance. The defect

[1] In Furness' Variorum Edition of *Hamlet* : " Through pity perceiving ".

is variously described in the *Hamlet-Litteratur*, " weit hergeholte Bedenklichkeiten " (Schlegel),[1] " overbalance of the contemplative faculty " (Coleridge),[2] and perhaps most important of all, in view of its treatment by modern critics like Bradley and Schücking, Vischer's [3] " melancholische Veranlagung."

The form taken by the theory has constantly altered, Bradley [4] in particular having shown how inadequate are the earlier views of its supporters. But two objections remain valid against all its forms. Firstly, irresolution is not of necessity consequent on any of the defects yet specified. Secondly along every path but one—that which leads direct to the king—Hamlet appears capable of instant and

[1] Schlegel (F. W.) *Vorlesungen über dramatische Kunst* 1809 : " far-fetched scruples ".

[2] Coleridge (S. T.) *Lectures on Shakespeare.* 1808.

[3] Vischer (Th.) *Kritische Gänge*, Heft 11. 1861 " melancholy disposition ".

[4] Bradley (A. C.) *Shakespearean Tragedy.* London, 1904.

vigorous action. It has yet to be shown that such a defect as " over-reflection " or " melancholy " *can* paralyse will. But even if we granted the consequence, we should still expect that a will " sicklied o'er by the pale cast of thought " or, to take the best description of this class, " crippled by melancholy," to betray a general and not a specific paralysis, or an explanation from this school of the factor or factors which make this paralysis specific or apparently specific.

Bradley, the latest and most important exponent of this school, finds in " a state of profound melancholy " the ultimate cause of delay, and the state is induced by " special circumstances," namely, the shock of his mother's remarriage. He realizes, of course, that such a shock could never in itself account for Hamlet's irresolution ; it takes effect only because Hamlet is predisposed by " an exquisite moral idealism " and by a temperament " the Elizabethans would have called melancholic."

Now from this predisposition which

Bradley describes, we can dismiss the element " exquisite moral idealism " as a factor in the delay. For, as Schücking[1] points out : " Though we admit that the outbreak of Hamlet's melancholy is evidently caused by his great disappointment at the marriage of his mother, yet we maintain that this kind of circumstance might have affected another kind of character possessing maybe as much or even more moral idealism, quite differently. It is a well-known fact that the extent and degree of the reaction is determined by the emotional susceptibility, not by the moral idealism."

My deep appreciation of Bradley's work will appear in the course of this essay. But even if we grant that any particular kind of melancholy could cause the delay, how shall we distinguish the kind that does from the kinds that do not ? And what kind of melancholy is this (" Such a state of feeling is inevitably adverse to

[1] Schücking (Levin) *Character-Problems in Shakespeare's Plays* (translated). London, 1922

any kind of decided action ") that prevents Hamlet from speedily killing the king, but allows him to act with apparent freedom and energy in every other direction? " These displays of vigour " says Robertson, " do not consist with a pessimism so laming as to preclude revenge."

III

Fletcher[1], Klein[1], and Werder[2], reacting homœpathically to the temperamentalism of their day, created the so-called " Aufgabe " hypothesis, like Hamlet's own reason a chameleon, but implying essentially that the difficulties inherent in the task itself, or likely to arise out of its fulfilment, were sufficient to deter anyone, however resolute, from accomplishing it.

[1] In Furness' Variorum *Hamlet*: " Task ".
[2] Werder (E.) *Vorlesungen über Shakespeares Hamlet*. 1875.

Hamlet's revenge as a public arraignment and degradation of Claudius may be found in Werder, but not in Shakespeare. Nor does the play reveal any concern on Hamlet's part at the prospect of banishment or execution, on a charge of murdering and slandering Claudius with intent to seize the throne. Claudius anticipates our distrust of such a theory by emphasizing on two occasions the general favour and esteem in which Hamlet is held by the people, and the refutation is completed in ironic tones by the ease with which Laertes arouses the " false Danish dogs." The people hail him king who has but one claim to the title—the will, as he takes it, to avenge a murdered father. We must conclude that external difficulties, though they would naturally be taken into account by anyone in Hamlet's position, cannot in themselves explain his peculiar hesitation.

IV

Ulrici[1], I believe, followed by such critics as Liebau[2], Mézières[2], Gerth[2], and Baumgart[2], was the first to suggest that Hamlet suffered from an inner conflict due to doubt as to the moral justification of the deed. The crop of this and related hypotheses was cut by Koenig's[2] famous 1873 statement: " Especial emphasis should be laid on the fact that nowhere in his numerous speeches does Hamlet intimate that he feels himself restricted by any definite consideration, by an external hindrance, or by any moral scruple." Ulrici and others tried to escape this flail by planting their seeds a little lower. Hamlet, they said, has no clear-cut ethical objections, but only a deep vague moral feeling or cultural prejudice that takes no definite form in

[1] Ulrici (H.) *Shakespeares Dramatische Kunst.* 1839.
[2] In Furness' Variorum *Hamlet.*

consciousness. Bradley shows how inconsistent is Shakespeare's treatment of Hamlet's duty with such an explanation, and Loening¹ retorts brusquely : " Handelt es sich um einen Konflikt zwischen der von aussen gebotenen Rachepflicht und einer inneren sittlichen oder rechtlichen Gegenströmung, so muss dieser Zwiespalt und seine Ursache bei einem so denkkräftigen und ans Denken gewohnten Menschen wie Hamlet zur Reflexion gebracht werden."

V

" The case indeed is this : had Hamlet gone naturally to work, there would have been an end of our play. The poet therefore was obliged to delay his hero's

---

[1] Loening. *Die Hamlet-Tragœdie Shakespeares.* 1893 : " Were it a question of a conflict between the obligation of vengeance urged from without and an inward moral opposition, it must have been perceived by a being of Hamlet's mental power and habit ".

revenge, but then he should have contrived some good reason for it."

A less tolerant criticism than that of Hanmer[1] has developed this view of the delay a sa fault in construction, and hence inexplicable. Robertson (1919)[2] succeeds Rapp[1], Rümelin[1], and Benedix[1] as its latest supporter. The delay is inexplicable because Shakespeare's "transmutation of the play was but a process of making more and more mysterious a delay which in the earlier stage was not mysterious at all", and " the revenge of the refined Hamlet must be delayed as was that of the barbaric Hamblet, without the original reason; the old machinery must be retained, down to the prayer-scene " . . . " A marvel his (.i.e., Shakespeare's) tour de force remains; but no jugglery can do away with the fact that the construction is incoherent, and the hero perforce an enigma, the snare of idolatrous criticism."

[1] In Furness' Variorum *Hamlet*.
[2] Robertson (J. M.) *The Problem of Hamlet*. London, 1919.

That the delay and the perplexity it involves are partly determined by the conditions of an older play, in which the delay was clearly essential, it has been no small service to Hamlet research for this school, and in particular for Robertson, to render. But can we, taking the play as a whole, and remembering its effect on the modern world, judge *Hamlet* without the Prince of Denmark, and dismiss it as a tour de force ? For what do we mean by the " Hamlet " enigma ? We are not affected by *Hamlet* because it baffles us, but we are baffled by it because it affects us so deeply and we cannot tell why. A mere fault in construction could never move us so. The delay is an integral part of the whole experience ; this it is that makes Loening's shoemaker turn analyst and this that inspired Grillparzer's [1] dry rejoinder to those of his time who asserted that the mystery was inexplicable " Dadurch wird

[1] Grillparzer (F.) *Studien zur Literargeschichte.* 1880. " Thereby it becomes a faithful representation of great events in this world, and achieves their colossal effect ".

es zu einem getreuen Bild der Weltbegebenheiten und wirkt ebenso ungeheuer als diese ".

Robertson, unlike many of his predecessors in this school, seems to realize the force of such objections as these when he says : " Utter sickness of heart, revealing itself in pessimism is again and again dramatically obtruded as if to set us feeling that for a heart so crushed revenge is no remedy. And this implicit pessimism is Shakespeare's personal contribution, his verdict on the situation set out by the play. But the fact remains that he has not merely not been explicit—as he could not be—he has left standing matter which conflicts with the solution of pessimism : he has exhibited Hamlet aroused to determination by the spectacle of the march of Fortinbras and declaring that he knows not why he has refrained ; and he has further exhibited him acting with abundant vigour in the sea-episode, as he had previously done in planning the Court play. These displays of vigour, like the killing of Polonius, do not consist with a pessimism so laming as to preclude revenge."

It is merely to the *insufficiency* of Bradley's solution that Robertson objects. The theory, then, of a defect in construction, especially as put forward by its latest supporter, is to be accepted as a supplement to Bradley's theory, but not as a substitute for it. A motivation in character still remains.

VI

Baumgart's objection " Das was ihn—Hamlet—an der Rache hindert ist ihm selbst ein Problem und deshalb musste es für uns alle ein Problem bleiben "[1] has been met in another way; the reason is

---

[1] That which prevents Hamlet from fulfilling his revenge is a problem to Hamlet himself, and therefore must remain a problem to all of us ".

unconscious to Hamlet but none the less real. Clutton-Brock,[1] for instance, sums up Hamlet's delay in a " formula " :

" The formula is this : That when Hamlet was implored by his father's ghost to avenge his murder and in particular to put an end to the incestuous marriage between his mother and the murderer, his conscious resolve, made with all the strength of his will, was to obey his father. But the shock which he suffered on hearing of the murder and particularly of realising the full horror of his mother's remarriage, made, as it were, a wound in his mind which hurt whenever he thought of the murder, or of his uncle, or of his mother's connection with his uncle. The pain of the wound was so sharp, that, unconsciously he flinched from it and seized every pretext to forget it."

Not even the flavour of " repression " can conceal this réchauffé of the old shock hypothesis, long since discarded as unfit

[1] Clutton-Brock (A.) *Shakespeare's Hamlet.* London, 1922.

for intellectual consumption. One feels like speaking daggers, if using none. But let us meet these rescussors with complaints just as old as their prey. Would characters like Laertes or Fortinbras have been so affected? If not, what is the peculiar quality in Hamlet that makes him so susceptible to shock? The significant human factor—Hamlet's predisposition—is left as much in the dark as ever: the obvious accidental factor of shock is urged as an explanation.

A theory which claims a more serious consideration is that put forward by Freud[1] (1906) and developed by Jones[2]. Freud's suggestion seems to have been unnoticed or ignored by the recording angels of *Hamlet*-criticism. Perhaps the view of Clutton-Brock, which " does not substantially differ from that held by wellnigh all æsthetic critics of repute "

---

[1] Freud (S.) *The Interpretation of Dreams*, translated by A. A. Brill. 1913.

[2] Jones (Ernest) *Das Problem des Hamlets und der Oedipus Komplex.* Vienna, 1910.

(Lee)[1], has satisfied their craving for a " psychological " solution.

Freud follows Bradley in taking Gertrude's remarriage as the first instance of Hamlet's trouble, though the shock of the ghost's revelation is its real precipitant. The element in Hamlet's predisposition which is affected pathologically by this shock is not a " melancholy temperament ", but the unconscious sexual fixation on the mother which is for Freud the determinant of most male neurosis. Jones, supporting Freud, points out that Gertrude is of just such a weak, stupid, and voluptuous nature as to have unwittingly corrupted from Hamlet's childhood an attachment which, though doubtless pure and holy to the conscious Hamlet, reveals in the play an excessive strength. He finds in Hamlet's attack on the king's lust in the bedchamber scene, a denunciation of sensuality so peculiarly sensual in itself, and in Hamlet's

---

[1] Lee (Sir Sidney), in *The Year's Work in English Studies*. London, 1922.

trait of effeminacy, a strong confirmation of Freud's view.

The fixation on the mother is accompanied from childhood by a hostile attitude, also unconscious, to the father, who is apperceived as a rival. Hamlet is predisposed, says Freud in effect, by a kind of double unconscious wish, of which a desire for the death of the father is the latter component. This desire is suddenly and accidentally fulfilled by the death of the elder Hamlet, and the former component presses forward for a like realization in consciousness. Hamlet is at once plunged into an unstable nervous condition by the need for " repression." The turmoil is increased by two external factors. Jones believes Hamlet to have been really rejected by Ophelia, and the effect of such a rejection, though it is chronologically the second factor, may be dealt with first. The attachment to the mother is strengthened by it, for the " libido " normally directed towards Ophelia falls back again to the old position from which it has so hardly escaped. The second factor is the effect of Gertrude's remarriage. Claudius is not only apperceived as a father-substitute by Hamlet, but is regarded with open loathing, for now he has no conscious filial piety to hem his unconscious hatred, but only a moral restraint.

This last restraint is removed by the ghost, and Hamlet's inner conflict begins. He is urged to a revenge which, if fulfilled, drags madness in its train, for to kill Claudius means to realise in consciousness the old childhood wish, one element fulfilled, and the other pressing for a like fulfilment. Whilst every reminder of his task fills him with remorse, it stirs up simultaneously this double wish, and Hamlet's conscious energy is immediately exhausted in keeping it from consciousness. Hence he is only released from the dilemma by the death of Gertrude. " Es ist kein blosser Zufall " (says Jones) " wenn Hamlet von sich selbst sagt, dass er ' by heaven and hell ' zur Rache angetrieben werde, obwohl ihm die wahre

Bedeutung dieser Phrase begreiflich-erweise entgeht"[1]

VII

The nature of the case precludes, of course, that we can accuse Freud and Jones of an arbitrary interpretation because their account has so little support from the text. Nor shall I avail myself of another charge that might be brought against them—that they confuse in their theory, art and reality.

"How can we discuss the effect on Hamlet" may cry some Schückingian critic " of childhood experiences not mentioned in the play? Hamlet was created to fit an action; outside that action he has no existence. How then can we speak of his past except where the poet precedes us?"

---

[1] "It is no mere accident," says Jones, " when Hamlet says of himself that he 'is driven to revenge' by heaven and hell ", although the real meaning of the phrase escapes his perception ".

Such an objection loses its force however, when we construe the Freudian theory, not as an absurd diagnosis of a fictive character, but as it was doubtless intended—a powerful analogy: " A person in real life, predisposed to an Oedipus Complex neurosis, and finding himself in circumstances similar to those of Hamlet, would delay just as Hamlet does." Bradley's theory might be likewise stated: the second clause now reading " with a predisposition the essential features of which are " melancholy " and " moral idealism."

Does this new predisposition " to an Oedipus Complex neurosis " suffice to explain the delay? According to Freud a sexual desire for the mother and a hostility to the father synchronize as a temporary and unconscious phase in the sexual evolution of all males. The difference between the " normal " and the " Oedipus Complex neurotic " lies in the more or less complete success of the former in passing beyond this stage, in freeing himself from desire for the mother by finding a new love-object outside the family, and in reconciling himself with the father or with father-surrogates (authorities etc.). The " Oedipus Complex neurotic " can never achieve such successful detachment, his " libido ", if checked in new orientations, is liable to " regress " to the former " family-situation ". Should he suffer " privation ", his " libido " slips back to a stage in its development forbidden to consciousness, and the struggle to " repress " this reactivation of old unconscious motives must end in neurosis.

It is not, therefore, in the possession of unconscious incest-fantasies, appearing disguised and distorted in dreams etc. that the " Oedipus Complex neurotic " differs from the Freudian " normal ", but in the degree in which the former is attached to them. " Libido-fixation ", says Freud, " represents the internal predisposing factor, whilst privation represents the external accidental factor in the aetiology." (*i.e.*, of neurosis).

Let us cede this position to the Freudians, reserving our verdict as to whether they have established their right to it or not. But in the interests of our desire for a fuller explanation of the delay we are entitled to ask: "Why then should the 'normal' be free from his fantasies and the 'neurotic' attached to them? What element is there in a character like that of Hamlet to attach it to a supposed phase of sexual development, when another character, even when subject to adverse circumstances like the death of the father or the continued 'spoiling' of the mother, can pass freely beyond this phase and never 'regress' to it? What, in short, is the factor that determines 'fixation' in the case of a character like that of Hamlet?"

The only description which Freud can offer us of such a factor is "a certain sexual constitution". But how this neurotic "sexual constitution" differs from that of the Freudian normal we are not informed, nor of the manner in which it effects a "fixation". The decisive factor, therefore, in the predisposition of a character like that of Hamlet to delay is still obscured for us and the solution of Freud and Jones reads in effect: " A person in real life, having a certain sexual constitution, which differs in some unknown manner from the normal, finding himself in circumstances like those of Hamlet, would delay just as he does."

Nor can it be allowed that the " external accidental factor " of " privation " has been satisfactorily established from the play. It is at least an open question whether Hamlet ever loved Ophelia at all. In fairness to Jones let me say that Hamlet's later attitude to Ophelia (for example in the nunnery-scene) is explained by him as a result of Hamlet's " Oedipus Complex neurosis " in a way which is thoroughly consistent with the rest of his theory. But Hamlet's desire to return to Wittenberg at the very beginning of the play and his silence in his soliloquies with regard to her are certainly opposed to the definite assertion that he really did love her at one time. Schücking, discussing such affirmations, says: " Gertrud Landsberg has very aptly shown that all these explanations based on subjective impressions can be more thoroughly tested by referring them to the dramatic history of this love-affair. She proves that in the German Hamlet— " Fratricide Punished "—which is probably to be regarded as a crude and distorted copy of the model which Shakespeare used, there is no love-affair worth talking about. We are even compelled to suppose that in the play which Shakespeare took for his starting-point Ophelia, so to speak, formed part of the other side. She is not, or at any rate she is no longer, his friend, but belongs to the royal party who are his enemies."

" Why is the delay specific ? " I asked, in discussing Bradley's theory. Jones finds that the decisive actions of Hamlet are vents for his " repressed hostility ", and, by a permutation of his " complex ", Laertes and Polonius are viewed as " rivals " for Ophelia. Rosencrantz and Guildenstern,

Osric and even the pirates too, I suppose, must join the Gilbertian chorus as " substitutes for fathers and for brothers ".

VIII

I have still to consider the valuable conclusions of two modern theorists, in my brief estimation of Hamlet research. These theorists, working in apparent independence of each other, have nevertheless many points in common. To Stoll[1] and to Schücking[2] the interpretation of Shakespeare should proceed not in the light of our time and our complex ideas, but in that of the Elizabethan era and the actual stage conditions in which Shakespeare worked. " The psychological, the morbid Hamlet, the realistic Hamlet, so

[1] Stoll (E. E.) *Hamlet : an historical and comparative study.* Research publications of the University of Minnesota, 1919.
[2] Schücking (Levin L.) *Character-Problems in Shakespeare's Plays* (translated). London, 1922.

to speak, is, we must conclude exclusively the discovery or invention of the ' Romantic Age ' ", says Stoll, and adds: " The present Hamlet theory arose and was developed far away from every tradition and echo of the stage by professors in a country where the theatre was anathema, and by Goethe who saw in him a sentimental version of his own Werther, and who was completely ignorant of the conditions of the Elizabethan stage."

When we look at the stage of Shakespeare from any viewpoint but that of the Elizabethan hind, we suffer from a kind of longsightedness. Passages which baffle the skill of our most able investigators must have been perfectly clear to the groundlings. And I agree that the Elizabethan audience, notwithstanding its importance with respect to the drama of its time and the new exegesis of ours, has not only been neglected by Shakesperean investigators in general, but has been deliberately obscured by the majority of them. The contours of this audience, once heavily marked, have been gradually lost in a fog of subjective criticism. No Loki has lightened their Nibelheim, but every philosopher has added generously of his darkness, and moistened its mists with his successful introspections. The flashes and tones which would mark such an audience under normal conditions have become in this gloom mere will-o'-the-wisps and muffled noises. How strange then sound their voices when they reach us at all, and how easily and wilfully mistaken are their more coherent expressions by careless and dishonest critics. Their deepest utterance, when naturally provoked, is as free and effective as that of any animal in contact with nature. But when this their birthright is lashed out of them by Hegelian Alberiches—it is callously welcomed as Weltschmerz.

To return to the delay. Stoll, forgetting for a moment such incidents as the bedchamber and nunnery scenes, and the double reason for the affront to Laertes, gives us a Hamlet who is " a gallant gentleman "—" the typical hero of a typical revenge-play" and "an heroic not a pathetic figure", in place of the shuffling and absent-minded philosopher, the prince of the clinic, the " sexual psychopath, obsessed with lust and incest" (Croce)[1]. And he finds in support that the importance of the delay has been greatly exaggerated, arguing, for instance, that the soliloquies show practically no trace of self-reproach, irresolution, or self-deception. In face of the work of Coleridge and of Bradley this latter conclusion certainly seems to derive its impulsiveness from the era in which Stoll shows himself such a master. He continues : " For Shakespeare the real and only question is how the tragedy shall remain a tragedy and at the same time the hero act like the gallant gentleman he is and yet not be a fool." And so " neither Kyd nor Shakespeare really motived it (*i.e.*, the delay), that is, grounded it in character." Yet two pages later he admits

[1] Croce (Benedetto) *Ariosto, Shakespeare, and Dante :* translated by Douglas Ainslie. London, 1920.

that " there are, here and there approaches to psychology, and what may at least seem a psychological motivation."

The doubt of the ghost and the reason for delay put forward by Hamlet in the prayer-scene are both urged as real by Stoll, and offered as important reductions of the delay-problem. I am as eager as he for such reductions, and agree that the delay has been exaggerated out of all proportion. But it seems to me that much of the work of this school is based on a false assumption—that no other interpretations of particular passages can co-exist with their own. Herford[1] makes my objection clear when he argues that Iago's admission of villainy is not only direct information for the audience (Schücking) but an expression of Iago's cynicism. In this particular case Bradley anticipates and advances upon Stoll's position by showing that Hamlet's hesitation in the prayer-scene is thoroughly consistent with the Elizabethan desire to

[1] Herford (C. H.) *Recent Shakespearean Investigations*. London, 1923

kill Claudius, body and soul. His objections, also, to the view that the doubt of the ghost was real, have still to be met by those whose only support for this view is derived from the currency, in Elizabeth's time, of a belief in ghosts as evil spirits. " Nothing, surely, can be clearer ", says Bradley, " than the meaning of this famous soliloquy. The doubt which appears at its close, instead of being the natural conclusion of the preceding thoughts, is totally inconsistent with them. For Hamlet's self reproaches, his curses on his enemy, and his perplexity about his own inaction, one and all imply his faith in the identity and truthfulness of the Ghost. Evidently this sudden doubt, of which there has not been the slightest trace before, is no genuine doubt ; it is an unconscious fiction, an excuse for his delay—and for its continuance."

And it seems strange, even in the restricted light that Stoll allows, that Shakespeare should have intended Hamlet's doubt of the ghost as real in view of the approaching confirmation of the Mouse-trap. Such a doubt would serve them no purpose, except as a temporary exhibition of an Elizabethan belief, and we should be forced to conclude that Shakespeare was working " step by step ", as Grillparzer puts it, in a place where such methods would attract notice as bad workmanship. We should expect too, that if the doubt were real, Hamlet would have offered it as an excuse to the ghost when it reproaches him for the delay in the closet scene. If the doubt is taken as unreal, however, it serves then a useful end in developing our impression of Hamlet's irresolution.

Considerations like the above lead to the conclusion that whether Shakespeare consciously intended Hamlet as "the typical hero of a typical revenge-tragedy " and created him in compliance with the whims and beliefs of the Elizabethan era or not, he has somehow created an immortal and universal figure, requiring every interpretation that can be applied to him, and not that of the groundling alone. An exegetic method, which demands a rigid interpretation of the text according to Elizabethan standards only, and which refuses the modification of any other interpretations, will explain Shakespeare's purpose just so much and insofar as it explains Shakespeare's attempt to adapt his art to the demands of those standards, and can explain it no more and no further. As a basis for the simplest possible interpretations, as a corrective to those that are forced, as a test or a partial or entire substitute for subjective ones, the method is highly valuable. The danger in its use lies in its interpretations being accepted as complete in themselves and exclusive of others which can really co-exist with them.

Schücking shares many of Stoll's basic principles. But the same method, the same objective data, the same confinement to the Elizabethan era, which almost create in themselves the Hamlet that Stoll introduces, the " hero " and " gallant gentleman " dashing through five acts to his triumphant revenge—issue through Schücking in a peeved and decrepit figure, "an imaginative brooding intellectualist with morbid traits", in whose nature "the first principle" is "weakness and irritability" and whose utterances, big with bile only, "were certainly received with laughter by the ordinary Elizabethan audience".

Now the historical realists have made a Gargantuan effort to raise from the frush of succeeding ages the Elizabethan era. They have not only re-created the atmosphere of Queen Bess, they have accustomed themselves to it. The forgeries of a modern exegesis, subtle and highly-wrought, broke to bits in their hands—they had to beat out their gear on Elizabethan anvils. Their reward is a method of research almost embarrassingly simple and honest. But, even with an exegesis as free from the charge of subjective determination as that of the historical realists, a conformity in the results of different investigators which is absolute and exact is surely not to be expected. In any research of a scientific nature some margin for discrepancies is always allowed. To cavil, therefore, because a bulge in the Hamlet of Stoll is a hollow in the Hamlet of Schücking, or vice versa, implies a demand as impossible in its fulfilment as it is captious in its origin.

Schücking, in his view of the delay, approaches more closely than any other critic I have mentioned to that of my own. For him, too, the delay is not that of a man affected by circumstances somehow ignored or hidden, nor a dark phase in a behaviour otherwise clear, but the evidence of some element in Hamlet which is continually expressing itself in other ways. And this element further, is not distinctive of Hamlet, but of a *type*, descriptions of which are to be found in Burton[1] and in Overbury[2] as " melancholic ". The " melancholic temperament " is mentioned by Bradley in his outline of Hamlet's predisposition,

[1] Burton, (Robert) *Anatomy of Melancholy*.
[2] Overbury (Sir Thomas) *Works*, edited by Rimbault. London, 1856.

but whilst for him " the direct cause was a state of mind quite abnormal and induced by special circumstances ", according to Schücking Hamlet delays because " the melancholy type . . . is incapable of concentrated systematic activity. Hamlet too is unable to pursue a plan." And he is disgusted and lacks self confidence because " the melancholy character, more than any other, is *naturally* liable to give vent to self-reproaches and doubts, by means of which he stirs himself to action " (the italics are mine).

But Schücking's view of the delay in particular, and of Hamlet's behaviour in general, anticipates and supports a later stage of my essay ; and to that stage I must refer for its fuller consideration.

IX

The head of Janus rises from out every theory of Hamlet, one face revealing the philosophy of its author, the other expressing something of an explanation we would all accept, could we have it entire. How familiar in Hamlet theorists is a concern for the former aspect, an avoidance of the latter, in reviewing the work of their predecessors. Divide et impera ! An ideal theorist would be one who could separate, in previous theories, the constructive from the non-constructive, who could show, in the broader and deeper sense of his own work, that their faults were but faults in development, and their contradictions apparent only.

Now certain constructive elements in the theories I have reviewed seem to me to be essential parts of any explanation of the delay which aims at being complete. Thus the revision of an older play (Robertson), and circumstances which anyone would have to take into account (Werder). But there is a motivation in the character of Hamlet still to be explained, and the constructive interpretations of theorists like Bradley, Freud and Schücking are not only incomplete, but derived from separate standpoints, and expressed as it were in different senses. Evidently a foundation deeper and broader than those of all such theories is necessary, if we are to reinterpret and unite as far as we can the valuable suggestions of their authors.

X

Now if the motivation is still obscured for us, we have seen, nevertheless, something of the element in character from which it proceeds. The element is not peculiar to Hamlet. For Bradley it is a " melancholic temperament "—a term one might apply to Hecuba or to Bygmester Solness.

Schücking states that the delay is expressive of a definite character, and Stoll shows how common a feature it is in the behaviour of many heroes, classical and modern. In effect, the ultimate cause of Hamlet's delay is to be found in some element which is present in every character of a certain *type*.

XI

Such a conclusion suggests at once that there is a definite element, which, if present in any character, will react to circumstances to produce that behaviour which we know as tragic, and that character without this element will never express itself in tragic behaviour under any circumstances.

And one needs but few observations from real life to confirm this position. Of two men, ruined in a business crisis, one will fall into neurosis or perversion or even go mad and kill himself. The other will proceed with calm to the reconstruction of his shattered fortunes. Nor can any second simultaneous circumstance be alleged as the cause of the former and tragic behaviour. It is always possible to find a third character, subject to this second circumstance, whose reaction to the first is non-tragic. The most advanced form of this argument finds in some " privation " of instinct or combination of such " privations " the second simultaneous circumstance alleged as the cause of tragic behaviour. And I have no need to restrict the enumeration of instincts or instinctive tendencies which may be liable to such " privations " : if so desired, the tendency of some of our writers to continually increase the instinctive tendencies may be also viewed as instinctive. But of two persons subject to the same circumstantial " privations " at any moment—one falls into neurosis, perversion, crime, suicide—the other successfully " sublimes " the thwarted instinct. The supporters of such a second simultaneous circumstance are invariably compelled to fall back on a distinctive element in character, existing from birth in the hero, as the determinant of tragic behaviour; an element which they cannot describe or distinguish. Some hereditary instinctive constitution, they say, effects an " attachment" to infantile experiences which hinders a successful " sublimation." But what this constitution is, or how it differs from the non-tragic constitution or how it affects this " attachment " to past experiences, is not revealed to us.

I can now make clear my position with regard to the so-called " conflict " between " character " and " circumstance." I do not refuse to the determinists the possibility of viewing character as a complex of circumstances. I assert simply that at any moment when behaviour is being studied, all circumstances which determine that behaviour as tragic are antecedent to that moment, and must act through character and not on it. At that moment any circumstance acting on a character may increase or diminish the tragic in its behaviour, or may determine its path, but no such circumstance can determine that behaviour as tragic or non-tragic. The tragic in behavour is determined by a distinctive element in character, which exists from the origin of that character. The mask that shall fit the περιπ'τεια the hero must wear from the start.

XII

So far I have dealt only with the *behaviour* of character. But character expresses itself in an inner movement as well, apparent to us through introspection. This inner movement I shall henceforth include with behaviour under the term " action."

Character, then, expresses itself in action. But how is the tragic element expressed in it? I find the expression most distinct in one aspect of action: its purposiveness.

We are accustomed to the idea of this purposiveness. The philosophy indeed that could deny Ziehen's statement—"that voluntary and involuntary actions are constantly aimed at attaining a definite end"—would but hitch its wagon to one star more secret and remote. But philosophy, so far from denying it, has welcomed and adorned it from earliest times. Even if a goal for action did not exist it would be necessary to invent one, for the assumption of such goals has been an essential factor in the development of every philosophy. It is when philosophers have offered the goals they described as final for human action, and all-inclusive of it, that they have earned the derision of critics. But when such goals have been assumed for the purpose of explaining some measure of human action, and to a certain point, the assumption at least has been justified.

Now for my purpose I need only consider action to the point where the tragic becomes distinct from the non-tragic, and only enough of action to afford the distinction. I need, that is, an intermediate and incomplete goal.

"Pleasure" and "self-preservation" are descriptions of goals which some even accept as final for human action, and all-inclusive of it. The concept of "pleasure," Atlas of many a philosophy, has developed immeasurably within recent years. But there is no standard for pleasure-feelings yet established, and no perception or action whose effect does not vary with circumstance, causing now pleasure now pain. Pleasure, indeed, may be felt *in* pain (masochism). The confusion affects even our most primitive appetites, for cultural restraint involves the "pain" of abstinence.

"Self-preservation," too, is a concept of utmost importance. But action, as much and as far as I need it, goes around and beyond this goal. We adopt when necessary a certain arbitrariness (Fres-Meyerhof) towards it, and even perform actions in the pursuit of pleasure which are harmful to our welfare.

"Pleasure," then, and "self-preservation" are concepts too indefinite or insufficient for my purpose. So I shall offer here as an abbreviated description of a goal which is placed at such a distance and includes such a volume of action as is essential to the distinction I desire, the term "*security*," and I shall consider action henceforth only insomuch and insofar as it is directed towards the goal which this term describes.

XIII

I shall offer no formal definition of this term "security." Its meaning, and its use in explaining the tragic, should become more precise in the course of my essay. But if any immediate reason were demanded for the assumption of such a goal

—one which appears now identical with the goal " pleasure ", now with the goal " self-preservation ", but which is really more sharply defined than the one, and includes a wider range of action than the other—surely our first impressions of the hero's conduct on the stage and in real life are of a person in some way feeling " insecure " in his environment, whether this " insecurity " appears to us as " pain " or " sense of danger ", and the " security " he desires some form of " pleasure " or " self-preservation ".

Indeed we can take it as a general rule that whenever action is tragic, the hero (*i.e.*, tragic character) acts as if he suffered a feeling of " insecurity ", bursting into magnificent tirade against " fate " on the stage, nervous, irritable, and preoccupied in life itself.

Non-tragic character, too, has its moments of " insecurity "—before examinations, decisions and the like. But reassurances assert themselves immediately, for non-tragic action tends always to preserve and strengthen a feeling of " security ". In this respect it has been shown by Vaihinger[1] that thought itself is continually subjected to the pressure of safety-tendencies.

The feeling of " insecurity " in tragic character seems somehow continuous, however, and on the stage we can see it become ever more intense as the action develops. By providing a series of situations which become more and more " insecure " for the hero the dramatist tries to convince us that these situations alone are responsible for his behaviour. The " inner conflict ", the feeling of " insecurity " of an Othello is due to the wiles of an Iago and an opportune handkerchief. The toil of circumstance weaves closer, our sympathy deepens, the " tragic flaw " is forgotten, the hero is crushed yet supreme, " universal man " battling with " overwhelming fate ", an immortal Laokoon.

We have seen, however, that circum-

[1] Vaihinger (Hans) *The Philosophy of " As If "*; translated by C. K. Ogden. London, 1924.

stances acting at that moment can never produce the feeling of " insecurity ", in his reaction to which the hero is tragic. Nor can a second simultaneous circumstance, like some " privation " of instinct, produce it. The feeling of " insecurity " is somehow *characteristic* of the hero.

XIV

We have been accustomed, since Darwin's time at least, to the idea of an external compulsion as the force that has transformed a group of cells into a complex human organism. Now whether we accept this idea or prefer to join Lamarck and his followers in explaining our evolution as the development of a self-conscious and self-directive force, adapting itself to environment to fulfil some higher end, matters little, provided we realize that a force of some sort demands a close adaptation of function to environment, and that delicate nervous systems and structures have been supplied to make that adaptation as accurate as possible. When our functions are satisfactorily adapted to their environment, when their nervous systems register no demands which they cannot fulfil, when we are, as it were, in physical and nervous equilibrium with our environment, we have a vague and diffuse sense of ease which is most closely defined as a feeling of security.

But let us suppose a function, which, because of some fault in its organ or gland or systems of these can only act in a defective manner. The strain is taken up by its nervous system and is registered in consciousness as a feeling of *insecurity*.

XV

But a feeling of insecurity is not the final psychic result of defective glands or organs.

A gland or organ, however defective,

must preserve *some* kind of equilibirum with the outer world. Its deficient function must increase, though in an abnormal manner, until a balance is struck with the demands made upon it. In order to make possible such an increase, the defect and its nerve-tracts become surrounded by structures of an inferior texture, but which serve as *compensations* for the defect.

And similarly *psychic* compensations are required, for the feeling of insecurity to preserve with the outer world a *psychic* equilibrium. Additional traits of character are developed to win the increased security essential; these form the framework for an attitude to the environment, a " philosophy ".

XVI

Early investigators defined the feeling of insecurity as some kind of fear. Then Janet made an important advance by qualifying it as a " sentiment d'incomplétude."

But the first to realize that the feeling of insecurity was not that of a mere organism, but of a human being moving in an economic, mental, social and moral existence as well as in a physical one, was Adler.[1] He showed that a vague and diffuse feeling of insecurity becomes sharply defined for its owner by his apperceptions of the society around him

XVII

I have said that the goal of action is security. But there is a force working through our society which tends continually to narrow and intensify this goal to one of a special kind of security—" superiority ". In spite of the security which love or pleasant work or health may grant us in the present, we find at times (and the frequency varies, of course, with the

[1] Adler (Alfred) *Studien über Minderwertigkeit von Organen.* 1907.

individual) that our action is narrowed and projected towards some " superior " position in life or in art—more money, better health or social standing, fuller powers of expression.

Such a goal does not dominate our lives, of course. We are only occupied with it at times, and even then we adopt a somewhat arbitrary attitude towards it. But one who feels insecure because of some unknown organic or glandular defect, takes this goal in a much more serious manner, and regards it almost incessantly. Because of his greater need, he naturally seeks security in well-defined forms, forms he can *grasp*, as it were, and just as a starving man sets a value upon bread which is economically false for well-fed people, so he, in his way, sets a " false " value upon a superior position in life or in art. Security becomes synonymous with success for him. Other people, occupied at times with the same end, are viewed by him as rivals who never cease the struggle. And so he seeks for incentives to urge himself onwards—

and finds them in his feeling of insecurity itself. In some way or other he feels handicapped, and, ignorant of the fact that his lowered self-esteem is due to glandular or organic trouble, he blames his indolence, his bad memory, his poverty, etc. And in consequence his feeling of being insecure becomes a nucleus for sensations and ideas which remind him continually that he is not so vigorous, clever or charming as other people, and that greater and more sustained efforts are required of him if he is to surpass them in any given direction. His feeling of being somehow insecure becomes sharply defined for him by this process as a feeling of *inferiority*. This is the specific quale of the hero.

XVIII

And the elevation of his uncertainty into what one might call his social consciousness, his sense of relation to men and affairs, and his awareness of their effect on him, needs psychic compensations at that level, just as his basic feeling of insecurity, which we assumed for a moment unaffected by apperception, had need of them. A feeling of inferiority is intolerable, and the hero makes all possible attempts to escape it or overcome it by acting in what he thinks is a " superior " manner, and by directing his action towards a " superior " goal. These attempts, however, are continually thwarted or confused by compensations for the basis of his feeling of inferiority—a feeling of insecurity. Such primary compensations are traits of character like self-mistrust, submissiveness, timidity, which form the framework for a generally circumspect attitude to his environment. And these traits and this attitude are felt in turn by him as evident of his inferiority, provoking the development of secondary, overlying traits to hide them from consciousness, and to strengthen for him the assurance of a certain " superiority " in the present and an increased

" superiority " in the future. Secondary, overlying traits of this kind are arrogance, disparagement of others, boldness and cruelty.

The character of the hero is built thus of traits which contend with each other, and which predominate according to his unstable need—now for caution, now for " superiority ". Hence the familiar contradictions in his behaviour. Hence the bravado, whilst *omnia tuta timens*.

XIX

It might be expected that the inner inconsistencies of such a character as that of the hero would interfere with the normal satisfaction of instinct. For example, the interference with instincts now generally accepted as such, like those of hunger and the " herd " (Trotter[1]) in the case of

[1] Trotter (W.) *Instincts of the Herd in Peace and War.* London, 1916.

hypochondriacs and eccentrics. The peculiarities of these people can only be understood as preparations for some future goal of superiority. The hero makes continual use of auxiliary assumptions—that by training on certain cinder-paths he will win in his Marathon.

The most important of these auxiliary assumptions has been carefully elaborated for us by Adler [1] (1924). The hero apperceives the male in our society as superior. Woman is classed by him as physically weaker, of poorer mentality or shallower ideals and morals, and generally less fitted than man for the economic, the social, the intellectual " struggle ". He feels that to attain his end he must act in a thoroughly masculine manner. And so the fictive picture of a superior position which hovers constantly before him is frequently obscured and anticipated by that of a masculine ideal, the picture of a powerful and successful male. He acts now on an " as-

[1] Adler (Alfred) *Individual Psychology*; translated by Radin. London, 1924.

if" projection (Vaihinger) into the future, "as-if" to act in a "masculine" manner were a vital auxiliary in the "struggle" for a superior position.

Thus his feeling of inferiority is often sharpened, as occasion requires, into one of effeminacy, and his primary traits of caution, submissiveness and the like appear feminine to him and opposed in his consciousness to the secondary traits of recklessness, ambition, etc., which now take on masculine hues. So develops an urge towards being and seeming masculine (and a depreciation of woman as a kind of corollary) which is peculiar to the hero.

XX

"But surely if he holds fast to ideas like these, that all human relations are a struggle, and that woman is inferior, the hero is bound to come into conflict with reality?"

We must remember, however, that the element of struggle and the positing of goals of superiority are familiar features of our civilisation, and not the illusions or prerogatives of heroes. Everyone imagines at times such a society and posits such a goal for himself. The masculine ideal, too, is well-nourished in our society. A non-tragic character makes continual use of it as a convenient adjustment. " It aids him in attaching himself to our masculine culture " says Adler ; " yes, it furnishes the latter with a steady impetus towards masculization." Indeed, so long as the hero does not carry this masculine behaviour too far, he is assured, not of hisses, but of encouraging applause.

Further, it must always be borne in mind, that the masculine urge, with its consequent depreciation of woman, is only an auxiliary to the power-tendency of the hero. " Should the direct effort to act like a man be checked " says Adler, " it avails itself of a circuitous route in which event the rôle of the woman is overvalued, passive traits are strengthened, masochistic, and in men, passive homosexual traits emerge." The hero changes the means but not the end and though these means be " feminine ", the final position of power appears always masculine to him.

Reality, then, is not entirely opposed to the action of the hero. But when he *does* meet with opposition he clings all the tighter to his fiction. He is now faced by what he imagines is a hostile and powerful world ; this deepens his sensations of inferiority, and hatred sustains now his lust for success. The shocks of defeat simply alter his plans ; his attitude is, if anything, hardened by them.

XXI

A further objection can be anticipated here—that the feeling of inferiority seems in some persons non-consequent on, or independent of, organic or glandular trouble. We all know persons, suffering from terrible diseases, whose attitude to their environment seems decidedly non-tragic, and others who, though apparently in perfect health, nevertheless show all the usual attempts to overcome a feeling of inferiority. In the case of the first class, if we eliminated the possibility of a goal of superiority through " submissiveness " or " patience " or " suffering," we should find that these individuals were assured of an additional security in the increased love and care of those about them, in work that was recognised as valuable, etc., etc., and that they had learnt something of the logic of life with regard to their original irritability and their disposition to domineer. The tendency to overcome a feeling of inferiority would no doubt still exist, in spite of the increased security, but it would be diverted into such harmless channels as pietism and art.

And the second class, though apparently healthy even to their physicians, will always prove subject to some organic or glandular defect. They were not originally healthy; they have acquired " health " as part of their " progress ", but they invariably so arrange their systems of maintaining this " health " as to retain enough of their former sensations of organic or glandular deficiency to confirm, as it were, the feeling of inferiority essential to the attainment of whatever goals they have posited.

XXII

I have suggested so far that tragic phenomena are best understood, not as the results of some " conflict ", but as the expressions of a definite tragic character, having for its basis a feeling of inferiority whose organic and psychic roots are now known. This feeling is the ἁμαρτία or so-called " tragic flaw ", and is common to every hero. The " error or frailty " which is pointed out in various heroes, insofar as such an " error or frailty " is tragic, is not the flaw itself, but only an attempt to hide it or overcome it.

XXIII

Ibsen has given us one hero of whose ἁμαρτία even the organic roots are unmistakable, but as a rule the tragic in stage behaviour can only be traced back to a certain point, and not, as in life becomes frequently possible, to its definite origin. Always, however, the state of uncertainty which is its *psychic* basis, reveals itself in that behaviour.

Thus Hamlet's " nervous instability ", his " rapid and perhaps extreme changes of mood and feeling " (Bradley) are expressive of this state, which, when the hero begins to move among men and affairs, becomes one of faulty equilibrium with them. A wary aggressiveness shows throughout Hamlet's whole conduct, as if the external world were resistant and hostile. " Yet have I in me something dangerous." And then first develop frail covering traits, stretch like antennae out into the darkness, testing it delicately. The most sensitive of these detaches itself from the suspicion that protects and restrains it, and arises, fine and wavering, as a desire to measure himself with those around him. But the desire falters, doubt contracting it, and curls, as it were, to a question mark. " Am I a Napoleon or only a louse ? " Hamlet seems to ask, like the Raskolnikov of Dostoieftsky, not only in his soliloquies, but before every new situation, and his subsequent conduct is always an answer to this question, an attempt to settle the doubt that the world is too much for him.

XXIV

Hamlet's grief at his mother's re-marriage is no longer excessively deep in view of his peculiar character. It would affect him first as a terrible humiliation, both in the slur on his father's memory, and in the revelation of his mother's faithlessness and sensuality. He would feel put to shame before the eyes of the Court, which must have known something of the real nature of this marriage. The realization, too, that Gertrude had preferred the pleasures of an abhorrent union to the love and the care that he could afford her, would not only deepen his sense of degradation, but would threaten his self-confidence at its very basis.

A character like this, with its increased need for security, would have attached itself strongly to the mother from childhood. But there is no need to suppose that this attachment is an " unconscious " or "sexual" one (Freud). A character like that of Hamlet might "arrange" such an unconscious sexual attachment, a psycho-analysis might reveal such an arrangement, but it would still be merely an expedient for assuring himself, in a concise and forcible manner, of a continuous security, and should by no means deceive us as well.

And this attachment would be accompanied by the familiar disposition to domineer, the origin of which has been already described. The desire to assure himself of his superiority and of his masculine prestige would show itself in attempts, however kindly, to "rule" over the mother, especially after the death of the father, who would serve as a precedent in this respect.

Now the re-marriage of Gertrude would almost entirely destroy for him the position of certainty and supremacy to which he had won, and which he had so long held. His little empire of the family has perished; his masculine attitudes are now ridiculous, for the figure she presents is not that of a helpless, dejected widow, but of a bride, a mate, independent in her new love of the former benevolent despotism that had protected her. Sensations of effeminacy would sharpen those of humiliation, shame, degradation and self-mistrust which Hamlet already felt.

These sensations would be enormously strengthened and concentrated by his apperceptions of Claudius. If we are to believe Hamlet, the latter is " a villain " and " a king of shreds and patches ". Yet an impartial analysis of the play will reveal that Claudius is in many respects superior to his opponent. Schücking's description of his character reproduces so exactly my own impressions that I shall give it at length. " The objection urged against Julius Caesar, that his character is assumed to be quite different from what it appears in our eyes in his actions, unquestionably holds good in the case of Claudius, his behaviour not corresponding in the least with what we hear of him. The events supposed to have occurred before the beginning of the action reveal him as an almost incredible criminal. The ghost of the murdered king speaks of him as one ' whose natural gifts were poor to those of mine.' Hamlet's descriptions make him out a cunning voluptuary, a ' vice of kings,' ' a king of shreds and patches.' According to this information we should expect to find him a vile sneak, a scoundrel anxiously and suspiciously watching over the crown he has stolen, at the very least a man whom the great lie on which he has built his very existence as king has given an uneasy or an artificial air. All the more surprised are we, when first making his acquaintance in the great state scene (I. ii), by the most princely deportment with which he discharges the duties of his great office. In a magnificent, well-ordered speech from the throne, which is as distinguished for the greatness of the thoughts as it is manly, even majestic, in tone, he treats of the affairs of the state, and his own with complete assurance and apparently with a perfectly clear conscience. . . . It is certain that in reality all he says would necessarily be false, but in the drama hypocrisy would also *have to betray itself* in some form or other. Now Shakespeare has made no efforts whatever to express this hypocrisy. Attempts to discover the king's character behind his words spring merely from the most subjective imagination. . . . This view (*i.e.*, that the hypocrisy of Claudius shows itself in his intelligence and tact) rests on a naïve inability to distinguish between art and reality. . . . This assassin is not only one of the most tender husbands Shakespeare has drawn, but also a true altruist in his sympathy for an unfortunate girl like Ophelia, and a hero who claims our admiration by his intrepidity in dangerous moments, as when Laertes raises a mutiny. Against all this evidence we are asked to believe that the theatrical performance arranged by Hamlet has so stirred up the King's conscience that the whole moral depravity of his behaviour comes home to him (III, iii), and causes him to reflect on the "blackness of his bosom," to make to himself what we may call a full confession of his guilt:

> O, my offence is rank, it smells to heaven ;
> It hath the primal eldest curse upon't ;
> A brother's murder !

This is not very convincing. However much the qualities of this figure during and before the action may conflict, it is certain that we are presented with an extremely energetic and intelligent man upon whom the theatrical performance could hardly have this effect. Only quite unstable or broken characters would, under such circumstances, at such moments, plunge into prayer for the purpose of remorseful self-contemplation. Here also the primitive psychology of the model has been uncritically taken over. We see how Shakespeare with great equanimity works out what is demanded by the plan already contained in the story. A further consideration is that the action could not dispense with the prayer scene, inasmuch as it is the only means of giving the spectator the final confirmation, which is urgently required, that the events related by the ghost have actually taken place in the manner described. There is still another point of view from which Shakespeare may have regarded this scene : his purpose throughout his work is to make his villains recognise the culpable nature of their actions, and this is done in the King's monologue. We thus come to the conclusion that the parts of this figure are not all of one cast, but *are formed in accordance with the part each one has to take in the action.* . . . Shakespeare here evidently worked, as Grillparzer says, " step by step " and each single part manifests the tendency, which was fully described before, toward independence of the scene and heightening of the scenic effect."

Shakespeare, then, intended a majestic and courageous opponent to Hamlet, but this conception, so essential to the unity of the whole expression, had to be modified in accordance with the strict lines of the older play. Nevertheless, the peculiar relations between Hamlet and the king, relations of no ordinary hostility, become illuminated for us in a flash, if we combine with the brilliant analysis of Schücking our recollection of Hamlet's continual embarrassment in the presence of Claudius, his timidity, and his evasions. The king, in spite of Hamlet's detractions, the origin of which should be quite clear to us now, is apperceived by Hamlet as in many respects superior, more capable, and more masculine than himself.

XXV

It must remain at present an open question, as I have already indicated, whether Hamlet really loved Ophelia or not at any time during the action. Could I go for confirmation behind the frame of the picture, I might be tempted to suggest that to Hamlet she was simply an experimental " conquest," a tentative and innocent Don Juanism. And were my supposition correct, a character like that of Hamlet would certainly accept this " rejection " as a " defeat." For the hero always imagines love as a state of subjection for the one party, of supremacy for the other : equality and the security that follows from it imply for him the disappearance of love. " Car l'amour," says Proust —and here is the gist of the tragic in love— " ne résiste en aucun cas à la sécurité " (" Security is the death of love"). Further, his sense of being humiliated would be all the deeper after the " rejection ", because she is no Helena nor Beatrice, but, and especially as he sees her, of a weak, stupid and somewhat shallow nature.

Thus Hamlet's " state of melancholy induced by special circumstances " (Bradley) is more sharply defined for us as a natural feeling of inferiority, localized and intensified by factors like his apperceptions of Gertrude's marriage, Claudius and Ophelia, factors which could never actually cause that feeling, but which become in its evaluation of the first importance.

XXVI

The trait most strongly marked in the character of the hero is that of ambition, this being at once the strongest of all compensations for his feeling of inferiority, and his most vivid projection into the uncertain future, mapping out a definite path to what is for him security—a position of power.

I use the term " ambition " here in a much broader sense than it generally possesses. But let us restrict it for a moment to its usual signification whilst I continue my analysis of Hamlet. I have no desire to over-emphasize this aspect of his behaviour. But there seems to me no doubt that Hamlet was disappointed and annoyed by his removal from succession. The removal may have been temporary, though Hamlet does not take it as such (" You cannot feed capons so " and "While the grass grows . . . "). He speaks more than once of his ambition, and it has yet to be shown that his speeches cannot be interpreted at their face-value on such occasions (Schücking and Stoll), even if it were proved that they were also attempts at the same time to deceive others—conclusions which are by no means satisfactorily established. When Rosencrantz asks him the cause of his distemper, "Sir, I lack advancement" he replies. Now it cannot be shown here, even if we admit that Hamlet is only playing with the courtier, that he is not simultaneously expressing a definite tendency in his character. Why also should Hamlet tell Ophelia that he is " very proud, revengeful, ambitious " if not as direct information to the audience? Why should he put Claudius on his guard by such a statement, if his plan is to deceive the latter, unless this tendency had slipped his discretion for a moment? What puts the matter beyond all reasonable doubt, however, is his speech to Horatio (V, ii) where there is no necessity for deception. We are forced to conclude that the death of Claudius would be very welcome to Hamlet, not only as a requital of his father's murder, and because he loathes him as his mother's seducer, but because the event would yield him a position of eminence, with all the security it implies to a tragic character.

Hamlet's desire to ascend the throne would act, therefore, as a reinforcement to the prompting of duty. But this desire is the narrowest interpretation one could give of his ambition : a character like his would be urged on to kill Claudius by other forces, auxiliary ambitions one might call them, of which he himself is but partly conscious. We have already seen that the most important of all these auxiliary ambitions is to be a thoroughly manly person. This ambition fortifies the guiding line to power in his consciousness, " as if " to be completely masculine were an anticipation of the final victory. The influence of Gertrude and Ophelia in this direction has never been really estimated. His masculine prestige has been certainly lowered to the former, and possibly to the latter as well. The attitudes he has constructed since childhood to Gertrude have been suddenly crushed, he has been thrust into the background, and especially before Claudius, the cause of it all, does he feel his effeminacy. A character like that of Hamlet would make fresh attempts to restore his masculine prestige, and the assassination of Claudius, the Caesar of the village, would be the first assurance not only to himself but to the Court, and in particular to Gertrude and Ophelia, that the restoration had been accomplsihed in a satisfactory manner.

Every reminder of his inferiority and effeminacy would spur him on along the path to the king. Now Gertrude and Ophelia afford such reminders in their most irritating form. He despises the one for her sensuality, the other for her shallowness. They both appear stupid and weak to him, and in real life every gesture or speech they could make would go to compose for him a nucleus of ideas and sensations around the feeling of being inferior and effeminate from which he tries so hard to escape.

Thus the auxiliary force of ambition which urges on Hamlet becomes continually sharpened for him, as if he were saying to himself, " If I kill Claudius I shall have freed myself from my terrible responsibilities ", and then subordinately : " I shall win myself a position of power (security) ", and " I shall prove myself a man ".

XXVII

His hesitation along the path to victory is paralleled in the action of every hero. It arises from that basic inconsistency in tragic character whose origin I have described in Section XVIII. Traits develop from the feeling of insecurity, the strongest of them being cautiousness, which cripple every sustained attempt at reaching a superior end. " Acheronta movebo " shouts the hero, and then, as he stoops down to blow off the dust, he fears he is straining his heart. He will run the last lap of his Marathon first—then stops— *il faut aller a tâtons* —(" *one must feel one's way* "). A confusion within him makes ludicrous all his behaviour. Some traits reach out continually to what is for him the only ultimate safety—a position of superiority, with its corollary of masculine action. Others cling tenaciously to the safety of inferiority, being passive and effeminate, caution and deliberation. Even success would be feared by a character like that of Hamlet—for thrones imply responsibilities as well as privileges.

What then of Hamlet's " decisive " and " courageous " actions ? These are at best preparations for a contest he never dare enter, at worst mere skirmishes, caracoles round the lists. His nearest approach to the main battle is a stab through a curtain. The hero who follows with the cry, " I'll make a ghost of him that lets me," the ghost of his murdered father, who boards the pirates, and who grapples with Laertes at the grave, risks life and limb, it is true, but not the dreadful humiliation of defeat at the hands of Claudius, before courtiers like Polonius and Osric, and most terrible of all, the despised Gertrude and Ophelia. In such an event he would experience at their utmost intensity all the sensations of being inferior, weak, stupid and effeminate from which he had strained to escape. And in face of this danger Hamlet continually persuades himself of the limitations of his craving for power and of his masculine urge along the path to the king, by reproaching, abusing and deceiving himself, whilst allowing these tendencies almost free play along every other path, in physical dangers, in wit, in his scorn for people like Polonius and Osric, whom he views as inferiors, and in his triumphant and vindictive attitudes to Gertrude and to Ophelia. In this manner, by keeping to the by-paths, he succeeds in convincing himself and others of his superiority, whilst avoiding the annihilation of this fiction by a defeat on the highroad.

I shall supplement these remarks by a few observations drawn direct from the play.

XXVIII

Act I. Hamlet's first soliloquy is of importance as a striking revelation of certain tendencies which are typical of the hero. Thus, by shifting the accent of his disgust from himself to his environment, he escapes a bitter realisation of his own shortcomings. Further, " Frailty thy name is woman " is not only the first sign of a depreciatory attitude towards all that is feminine, but that of a severe view of moral lapses, more fully developed later.

" Such an act
That blurs the grace and blush of modesty,
Calls virtue hypocrite ".

The severity recurs in his attack on the

intemperance of his countrymen. Such a desire to play the moral censor, such intolerance towards the failings of others, is largely selfish in its origin. The hero is assured thereby of his own superiority and of the respect of others at the same time. " The melancholy character," says Schücking, " feeding his discontent with constant brooding and proudly fond of his loneliness, inevitably develops into a censor of morals, a function which he can, of course, exercise only if he takes a high ethical standpoint." Perhaps the Brand of Ibsen reveals this trait most clearly, though it is latent in every hero.

The revelation of the ghost affects Hamlet in such a dreadful manner because he realises at heart that he cannot fulfil the task, that he is inferior and unfit. He hastens to reassure himself that he is superior and adequate by a tremendous resolve :

> " And thy commandment all alone shall live
> Within the book and volume of my brain ",

by a fierce repulsion of the sudden

reminder afforded by Gertrude of his own effeminacy :

"O most pernicious woman!"

and by an attempt to convince himself that his general attitude of hostility towards mankind ("a disposition inimical to the world and to life".—Kuno Fischer) is a hatred of his uncle.

He hides his doubt and despair not only from Horatio and Marcellus, but from himself, by the assumption of a "masculine" carelessness: "Hillo, ho, ho, boy!" and so essential is the maintenance of this that he even carries its abandon into disrespect for the ghost.

As for Hamlet's "antic disposition", modern research tends to combine the view that Hamlet is really mad with the apparently opposite view that he is mad in craft only. Jones finds in the "antic disposition" the familiar Dummstellen of young children: the simulation of an air of innocence or stupidity by the enfant terrible in order to give free play to tendencies which would be otherwise checked or punished. " Aus meinen Psychoanalysen Neurotischer weiss ich ", says Freud, " dass die sogenannte Naivität junger Leute und Kinder haüfig nur solch ein Mask ist um das Unanstandige unbeirrt durch Genieren aussprechen oder tun zu können ".[1]

Thus Hamlet's " madness " serves him as a convenient disguise for an indulgence of triumphs in wit and action at the expense of those around him, especially Claudius. But madness is extremely difficult for any sane person to simulate for any length of time, the motive is always suspicious, and the ability to simulate it for long invariably proceeds from an actual mental derangement.

In short Hamlet is indeed only " mad north-north-west " but then—so are all other madmen.

[1] " I know from my psychoanalysis of neurotics ", says Freud, " that the so-called naïveté of young people and children is frequently a disguise for the unembarrassed expression in action or speech of what would not be tolerated under other circumstances ". *Zur Psychopathologie des Alltagslebens.*

XXIX

Act II. It is evident that many motives play through Hamlet's appearance to Ophelia (as described by her in sc. i) apart from his desire to deceive the court into supposing a false origin of his " antic disposition ". His conduct almost hints at an absurd burlesque, a mock examination and renunciation of all that is feeble, passive and effeminate, symbolised by Ophelia, as a preparation for his task.

His remarkable intolerance, and especially of Polonius, has been previously indicated. The irritation he feels against persons like these is due to the reminders they afford of his own inferior traits.

An impassioned self-disgust marks the beginning of the Hecuba soliloquy,

" O, what a rogue and peasant slave am I ! "

but he quickly swerves from the pain of

self-estimation to the grandeur and force of the wrongs which he suffers—

> " What would he do,
> Had he the motive and the cue for passion
> That I have ? "

—only to return slowly but with renewed force to his first consideration.

> " Yet I,
> A dull and muddy-mettled rascal, peak,
> Like John-a-dreams, unpregnant of my cause."

The primary aim both of his self-reproaches and of his reactions to them is to widen the scale of his ego-consciousness, his sense of the extremes in his own nature. We may note in such movements the fundamental unrest of all tragic character, the endless swing of its needle between two opposite poles.

The following lines show a similar sudden oscillation. Hamlet's realization of cowardice is followed by a violent attack on the king—

> " bloody, bawdy villain !
> Remorseless, treacherous, lecherous, kindless villain!"

and then the return swing, this time to the zero of all baseness and effeminacy.

> " Must, like a whore, unpack my heart with words,
> And fall a-cursing, like a very drab,
> A scullion ! "

XXX

Act III, sc. i. The soliloquy on suicide might be intended as an abstract of Hamlet's whole action. For here at its plainest appears the split in personality, the dual striving. The idea of suicide is attractive to all heroes: it is reserved as a grand finale to neglected existence. And then arises the feeling of humiliation in renouncing their personality, in turning to dust—and the old contradiction reappears.

Hamlet is occupied chiefly by the security from further humiliation which a dignified withdrawal might afford, though his passion for acting would no doubt find satisfaction in a startling " curtain ". But just as the dangerous task of revenge is obstructed by a cunning variety of pretexts, so, as protections against suicide, he calls up the dreams.

> " For in that sleep of death what dreams may come ".

" In what way are Hamlet's insults to Ophelia necessary to his purpose of revenge ? " asks Bradley. Yet these insults are not without aim in this direction. At first his contempt is for Ophelia only,

> " No, not I : I never gave you aught."

and the poor web she spins :

> " Indeed, my lord, you made me believe so "

is broken :

> " You should not have believed me, I loved you not "

hangs listlessly :

> " I was the more deceived ".

But the disparagement quickly becomes more general, blind and desperate blows at all that is woman :

> "Or if thou wilt needs marry, marry a fool; for wise men know well enough what monsters you make of them . . . you jig, you amble, and you lisp, and nick-name God's creatures, and make your wantonness your ignorance."

which serve to reassure him that he is manly, and capable of his task.

> "Go to, I'll no more on't; it hath made me mad. I say, we will have no more marriages: those that are married already, *all but one*, shall live."

The play draws near, the decisive test. "But how characteristic it is", says Bradley, "that he appears quite as anxious his speech should not be ranted as that Horatio should observe its effect upon the king". And, after the king has risen, "it is not the fearful evidence of the crime which occupies him at first", adds Gervinus, "but the pleasure in his skill as actor or poet".

> "Would not this, sir, and a forest of feathers—if the rest of my fortunes turn Turk with me—with two Provincial roses on my razed shoes, get me a fellowship in a cry of players, sir?"

And we must yield to the justice of Hamlet's boast. He does indeed resemble the ambitious actor : in every scene he strives for the " fat ". For the hero will excel in all directions. If he cannot surpass in joy or wit he will do so in grief or vituperation. If he fails as voluptuary, one can find him in sack-cloth and ashes, wailing with more force than any of the professional ascetics. So too in Hamlet's case. Doubting and fearing that he cannot reach his end, cannot master his task, his action continually comes to a short focus in the pettiest of goals—the desire to outdo, at any moment, the efforts of those around him, maintaining thereby his fiction of superiority both to others and to himself. He will be king among hamlets rather than prince in Elsinore.

Sc. iii. Hamlet comes on his uncle praying. " The first five words he utters : ' Now might I do it ', show that he has no effective *desire* to do it ". Bradley precedes me here with his usual fine intuition. For it is a definite characteristic of the hero that he cannot, as Kant puts it, eliminate his projections from his calculations.

Hamlet's pretext " Up, sword, and know thou a more horrid hent " betrays two important tendencies in his nature. The first is to postpone a decision, preserving thereby his own superiority (for he persuades himself that he is going to make a much better job of it) and, at the same time, avoiding the humiliation of a prospective defeat in the present. The second is " Hamlet's desire for the revenge perfect " (Hazlitt [1]), the passion for thoroughness that proceeds as a natural consequence from the hero's deep sense of incapacity.

Sc. iv. With regard to the prohibition broken so as to be couched in one part as a positive command, and the descriptive attacks upon lust in this scene, we should remember that a tragic character, with its poignant realization of deficiency, is bent on expanding its ego-consciousness and sense of power in every direction, even if

---

[1] See Furness' Variorum : *Hamlet.*

that expansion is downward and the sense of power merely that of libidinous tension. The hero makes constant use of his sensations of such a tension as a standard of reference, and the deception of analysts becomes easy. Hence the mistaken view of Freud and Jones that Hamlet here betrays a definite sexual fixation on the mother. Schücking reduces the whole matter in a commonsense manner to its correct proportions, when he says: " These things, *i.e.*, Hamlet's luxuriating in the minute descriptions of the sexual relations between his mother and his step-father, the warning he gives her not to

> " Let the bloat king tempt you again to bed;
> Pinch wanton on your cheek "

are either passed over by critics of Hamlet in silence as unfit for treatment, or made the pivot of the whole problem. Both conceptions are equally wrong. The indulging in erotic imaginations and the interest taken in procreation and the peculiar qualities of women, due to a feeling of disgust, are regular traits of the melancholy character."

XXXI

Act IV, Sc. i, ii, iii. Hamlet is evidently maintaining through the valuable *Dummstellen* the impression of moral irresponsibility, in his almost animal treatment of the body of Polonius.

Just as he escaped from the contemplation of his task by playing the homilist in the bed-chamber scene when he should have been occupied in winning his mother as his accomplice, so now he seizes with delight on the prospect of a contest of wits with Claudius, however temporary and futile the victory. His vital purpose is now but the innervation of a myriad antennae, a diffuse groping after the prizes of the moment. Had Claudius asked him to play chess instead—but this is going behind the frame of the picture.

Sc. iv. Hamlet's uncertainty of himself and his consequent constant self-comparison with others have been noted before in the Hecuba speech, and are again in striking evidence in the Fortinbras soliloquy.

"How stand I then . . . .

The theories of Schlegel and Coleridge obtain strong support from this scene. But these critics fail to perceive that his excessive reflection is merely symptomatic of a deeper trouble, as Bradley points out. To weigh and consider, to question and doubt, such are the devices of one who wishes to avoid the humiliation of defeat, the destruction, by the realities of the future, of the fictions that surround him like a protecting armour. His own inability to understand why he delays is not the least valuable of these devices.

We notice in this speech movements similar to those of the Hecuba soliloquy—

from the repelling realization of his own incapacity :

"Bestial oblivion, or some craven scruple"

—to reassurances of an almost physical violence :

"Excitements of my reason and my blood."

And the "recurrence of the identical" (Nietzsche) is nowhere so well marked as in the action of the hero.

A small point in Sc. vii is the king's mention of Hamlet's envy of Laertes' skill in fencing :

"Sir, this report of his
Did Hamlet so envenom with his envy . . ."

This falls into its natural place as an expression of Hamlet's general disposition to excel, and is supported by Goethe's curious observation "His zeal for knightly exercises was not entirely his own, not altogether natural to him ; it had rather to be quickened and inflamed by praise bestowed upon another."

XXXII

Act V. Throughout the action of Hamlet, an attitude towards " fate " that undergoes a continual evolution is in evidence.

"The time is out of joint: O cursed spite,
That ever I was born to set it right!"

Here is the usual mechanism in blaming "fate"; the realization of one's own shortcomings is avoided by shifting the responsibility.

There is a recurrence of the old honesty, though tinged with an ironic sophistication, in his remarks to Rosencrantz and Guildenstern (II, ii)

"I have of late—but wherefore I know not—lost all my mirth, forgone all custom of exercises; and indeed it goes so heavily with my disposition that this goodly frame, the earth, seems to me a sterile promontory"

but this is followed by admiration for one:

> "in suffering all, that suffers nothing ;
> A man that fortune's buffets and rewards
> Hast ta'en with equal thanks" (III, ii).

In all this we can see the attempt to rise above "fate", first by an attitude of disparagement, and then of a contemptuous stoicism. Before he leaves England the rigidity slackens a little : he shows signs of acquiescence with his lot after the murder of Polonius :

> "I do repent : but heaven hath pleased it so."

On his return to England, as Bradley points out, there is an undoubted development of this "fatalism". His mood is now one of careless indifference, he seems to have resigned himself to the eddies of his "destiny". Yet whenever the surface mood is broken for a moment, we glimpse once again the old unrest, the dual striving. He who believes that "since no man has aught of what he leaves, what is't to leave betimes ?"—how abhorrent to him is the skull of poor Yorick ! He is appalled that even the skull of an Alexander must look and smell " o' this fashion i' the earth "

His "fatalism" simply conceals the old instability; he is as ready as always to forsake the " safety " of non-action for the will-o'-the-wisps that ever hover before him. This is strikingly witnessed by his attack on Laertes at the grave of Ophelia. No love for her but for lime-light is its motive. " It is undoubtedly true ", says Schücking, " that later on, at Ophelia's funeral, Hamlet gets into a high state of excitement and in a mind of frenzy hurls his passionate love in the faces of the bystanders. Yet not only do they at once recognize his behaviour to be thoroughly morbid, but he himself afterward confirms this opinion by pleading in excuse of his conduct a momentary outburst of passion due to his madness (V, ii). Even if we do Shakespeare's technique so little justice as to see no reference to fact in this statement, we cannot shut our eyes to the perception that Hamlet in private conversation with Horatio (V, ii) sees these things essentially in the same way. He does not think for a moment of describing his behaviour to Horatio as due to any excessive pain caused by Ophelia's death. On the contrary he says not a word about her, but states expressly that " the bravery (*i.e.*, the ostentation) of his (*i.e.*, Laertes') grief" has roused him to a " towering passion" and thus brought about the " fit " (V, ii, 79). This account perfectly agrees with the peculiarity of the melancholy temperament, that its victim is infuriated by the idea that anyone else wants to be more unhappy than himself."

The " as if " projected line of conduct (Vaihinger) is particularly clear in this incident.

> " Rightly to be great
> Is not to stir without great argument."

He has avoided the question of revenge until Horatio draws his attention to it: even then the old need for reassurance shows as sharply as ever.

> "Does it not, think'st thee, stand me now upon—
> is't not perfect conscience
> To quit him with this arm?"

And it is only when he realizes that his own life is ebbing that he can at last perform his duty.

> The point envenom'd too . . ."

XXXIII

A few minor indications of the tragic in Hamlet call for a brief consideration. First we have the trick of repetition in speech, noticed by Bradley. "Very like, very like"—"I humbly thank you, well, well, well"—"except my life, except my life, except my life." The habit proceeds from a sense of the need of emphasizing his expression, as if he felt instinctively that without repetition it lacked in importance. It is a slight expression of a fundamental instability in character, and is also evident in Hamlet's punning, which assures him of his cleverness at the same time as it " mystifies, thwarts and annoys". (Bradley)

The same feeling of insecurity is responsible for the exaggerated contrasts of which Hamlet makes use. " Hyperion to a satyr " etc. The hero relies continually on thought of an antithetic form, antithetic analogies etc. He opposes " good " to " evil ", " masculine " to " feminine ", and so forth, grouping his ideas around two opposite poles of " superiority " and " inferiority ", in order to project a superior line of conduct. Thus comes into being a belief in the omnipotence of his thought (Freud). " For there is nothing either good or bad but thinking makes it so ". As Erda rises to console Wotan, so rises from his despair to the hero a radiant figure, one tender with hope, and saying like Erda :

" Mein Schlaf is Traümen
  mein Traümen Sinnen
Mein Sinnen Walten des Wissens."[1]

[1] " My sleep is a dreaming
     My dream meditation.
   My thinking the monarch of thought ".

XXXIV

Shakespeare's concern in this play seems to have been to put but one black figure against his highest white, for the tragic in the other characters of this play becomes slight in comparison with that in Hamlet. Yet these characters are *relatively* of great importance, and so evident is this in the case of Ophelia and Gertrude that one can induce as a general rule that the hero's apperception of the women who surround him becomes the most important factor in the evaluation both of his feeling of inferiority and of his inevitable attempts to overcome that feeling in what we know as tragic action. In the case of Hamlet the process is somewhat complicated by other factors; a clearer instance is afforded by the influence of Lady Macbeth on her husband.

"Good sir, why do you start, and seem to fear
Things that do sound so fair?"

The powerful effect of the three witches is not due, as some critics maintain, to the realization by Macbeth of secret and slumbering wishes, for such a realization might occur to anyone—Banquo for instance. Macbeth is predisposed to be so affected :

> " This supernatural soliciting
> Cannot be ill ; cannot be good : "

The bubble doubt on a spirit never level !

" Macbeth " has been particularized as the " tragedy of ambition ". It is not, however, a mere desire for the throne that carries him to destruction—this he views with equanimity :

> " If chance will have me king, why, chance may crown me
> Without my stir."

But the surface flow of ambition is continually reinforced by a swell from a deeper source, which Macbeth as continually dams :

> " I dare do all that may become a man :
> Who dares do more is none."

Lady Macbeth removes the restraints.

Perhaps the most concise illustration of woman's influence on the hero appears in the Solness of Ibsen. In the early stages of the drama, quite apart from such retrospections as the " crack in the chimney " episode, the hero already betrays the typical double characteristic in his ambition to surpass all rivals and in his fear of the " younger generation ". The dilemma in which he finds himself is only crystallized from its vagueness by the entry of Hilda Wangel. Through a careless one of her questions now throng all his scattered doubts and reproaches, as, on the best path up a mountain a great crowd might hasten.

> " That my master-builder dares not—cannot—climb as high as he builds ? "

Here in one sentence appears the hero's picture of woman, her attitude one of question, her air now idle, now provocative, and ironic doubt in her glances. By simplifying and symbolising, in however crude a manner, his fears and desires, she makes more real and insistent for him at once the uncertain past, the present suspense, and the victory of the future.

XXXV

The desire to " climb as high as he builds " and the dread of vertigo—so converge the old yearnings, the fears once so vague. And just as a secondary orientation develops towards Hilda, as if, when he had sworn to test himself, Solness had subordinately added " I will prove myself a competent lover to her "—so does every hero find need of a kind of preparation and auxiliary for his struggles in a definite attitude to the women around him, one which is the same to his own sensations of effeminacy. Direct disparagement, as instanced in the action of Hamlet, is the most usual of these attitudes. But the stress of the real and the refinement of purpose often compel a more subtle, one might say more aesthetic, orientation towards woman. Hence the extremes: Don Juan and Hippolytus. In art and in life they scamper so hurriedly from each other and assume poses so evidently in contrast that even the most superficial observer becomes gradually convinced that here are twins, each escaped from the same kindergarten.

Marbodius has shaped both their pedestals. " Femina, dulce malum pariter favus atque venenum."[1]

As a masculine kleine Gernegross Juan is the more apparent. He thinks of die Schönen im Plural in order to obtain, from the sequence of conquests, the gentle and reiterated assurance that he is masculine.

[1] " Woman, a sweet evil, honey and venom both ". " little Will be-Big ".

> " Du siehst, mit diesem Trank im Leibe
> Bald Helenen in jedem Weibe ".[1]

But as Helen explodes every time he embraces her, victory becomes defeat for him.

And the follower of Artemis, Hippolytus ? How shyly he draws from the beauteous snare :

> " Curse ye ! My woman hate shall ne'er be sated,
> Not though one say that this is all my theme."

Yet one more scene where love oppresses, the flower-scene from Parsifal. In all the falling flower-music stands one who is pure and erect, among maidens themselves like flowers. He heeds not the fragrant entreaty, the gentle imploring gestures—

> " Die Blümen lässt du umbuhlen den Falter ? "[2]

Rhythmic they sway, gently pleading around him, voices soft and hearts

---

[1] " Thou'lt find, this drink thy blood compelling,
    Each woman beautiful as Helen ".—(Bayard Taylor).

[2] " The flowers must woo the butterfly ? "

yearning, advancing hesitate—falter yet lingering.

Sudden his anger and like birds they break, hither—thither, crying—wondering.

"Lasst ab! Ihr fangt mich nicht!"[1]

The golden happy voice! Through the derision, silver of voices, echo languishes in echo.

XXXVI

A tendency latent in every hero presses for its complete expression in the pose of a "victim". For Mime must sing as well as Siegfried. The "victim" feels his inferiority as a kind of injury: "fate" and his environment have conspired to mar him. He has failed through the guilt of others, he says, and stands free from all responsibility. His aggressive impulses,

[1] "Away: Your snares are vain".

hiding his inferiority from himself and from others, he transfers with minute skill to all that surrounds him. " The little dogs and all, Tray, Blanch, and Sweetheart, see, they bark at me ". Lear shows from the outset a broken character. He wants to evade his responsibilities ; and yet he is so afraid to let go of his burden that he must demand pledges of love from his own daughters. Not only the immediate treatment of Cordelia and Kent, but the whole of his subsequent behaviour, betrays the familiar staircase regret of the hero, haunting his every decision, motivated as these are by fear and ambition. The " hostility " of Regan and Goneril is partly real, for they are both tragic characters—as for the rest " Der Unheil fürchtet were unhold ist ".[1]

The delight in misery of these people derives from an urge to maximate their ego-consciousness as a reassurance of some sort of power, and to convince the essential spectator of their superiority. " How

[1] " He who is hostile fears attack ".

wild is our wailing, our woe how deep" exclaims Hecuba. And the Siegmund of Wagner is franker still, ending the long recital of his wrongs with an epitaph for every "victim".

"drum musst' ich mich Wehwalt nennen,
des Wehes waltet' ich nur."[1]

XXXVII

A simple sketch of passive and masochistic traits would express what is tragic in Hecuba, but a delineation of the heroine is usually much more complex. She is naturally readier in her use of feminine methods to attain her ends, and masculine tactics are employed by her in a cruder manner. Vaihinger's work enables me to point out that she acts on an "as if" which strengthens the ego-line, assuming now masculine, now feminine as the only means to the goal she has posited.

[1] "Thus must I call myself being of woe,
  For woe alone did I rule".

Thus in Medea we have the tragedy of a woman who has been thrust into the background and another preferred to her. She forces herself to the front once more by showing herself more " masculine " than her rival, and by a terrible act of " masculine " cruelty, as if to assert herself, as if saying : " Weak and contemptible held'st thou me, one who has yielded to thee and borne thee male kind. See that as any man, I too can be fell ".

But this " masculine " triumph is partly obtained by a hoodwinking of Jason which a character like this—and the spectator too—apperceives as a " feminine " artifice :

> " but we, weak women, are
> What nature formed us ; therefore our defects
> Thou must not imitate, nor yet return
> Folly for folly."

The reason why the tragic in heroines affects us so deeply is because the appearance of effort is so much more intense. In the race with the male she feels handicapped, and in spite of her seeming indifference, is pricked on by the goads of despair. At heart she feels, her myriad steps now furtively hastening, now tripping ever faster, that however quickly she may race :

" Mit Einem Sprunge macht's der Mann."[1]

XXXVIII

The heroine is most fully expressed in the Hedda Gabler of Ibsen. Her father is a general, retired on a somewhat limited income, and Hedda is brought up in the society which shaped Captain Alving, a society of obvious, rigid ideals, and secret and supple vices. Genteel poverty and a dread of scandal limit her pleasures to dancing and the discreet admiration of a male entourage. Into this life comes Eilert Lövborg, a dissolute young genius, and between them there grows up an intimate friendship, though in a secret

[1] " Man in one leap has cleared the way ".—(Bayard Taylor).

and twisted fashion. For she, clinging timidly to her narrow ideals, must satisfy her cravings in curiosity, and in a warped curiosity at that, as not daring to commit herself to a direct inquiry, she must ask him " round-about " questions of a side of life still concealed to her. When Lövborg makes the inevitable advances, she reacts in heroic manner by threatening him with a pistol and driving him from the house, afraid not only of scandal, but of the force of her own impulses.

Finding her position uncertain among lovers who have a profound awe of the marriage-tie, she accepts as her husband one Jörgen Tesman, a mediocrity, but " safe " and respectable and submissive to her every wish. The play opens with the return from their honeymoon. Hedda crowds his Aunt Julia from her carriage by her pile of boxes. The old lady calls on her later, only to incur renewed insult through leaving her bonnet about.

After his " defeat ", Lövborg sinks to the position of tutor to the children of a

Sheriff Elvsted, who has found a wife cheaper than a governess and housekeeper. Mrs. Elvsted reclaims Lövborg, inspires him to new efforts, and helps him to write his books. But with his first success he leaves their household and comes to town. Fearing that he is backsliding, Thea Elvsted thinks that her duty lies rather in being an aid to a genius than a mere convenience to her selfish husband, and follows Eilert to town. She goes for information to the Tesmans (for not only is Hedda an old school friend of hers, but Tesman himself is a former fellow-graduate of Eilert Lövborg) and implores them to give Lövborg the social standing so essential to his self-esteem, informing Hedda in private of the work she and he have together. Judge Brack enters now, a former admirer of Hedda, but one who has tastes for a ménage à trois. He seems to be obtaining some financial hold over Tesman, and the act ends with an appeal from the latter that Hedda shall limit her expenditure.

XXXIX

Our impression is that of a clever, fascinating, insolent selfish and extravagant woman, afraid of convention, yet thoroughly dissatisfied with her narrow existence. She despises her husband as one of a lower caste, and treats his relations with short contempt. His flabby sentiment, his Privatdozent ideas, his sheepish and easy-going subservience affect her ad nauseam. Above all she feels herself crippled, with no room for development among people who cannot possibly appreciate her personality. She has acted with " cowardice " in rejecting Lövborg, and stupidly in accepting Tesman. And now she is bored to death.

Her sensations, ideas and reflections gradually harden about a feeling that her position is inferior, and her activities thwarted. And this feeling becomes intolerably acute in the consciousness of approaching motherhood. It is not only the repulsive physical crisis, the danger to her health that she fears, but the humiliation of bearing a child to the man she despises, and of being nursed by his insufferable aunts, of becoming one of the family indeed.

She covers her irritation by selfish, insolent and extravagant behaviour, and by flirting with Brack. But her terror of scandal restrains her here: she had one pistol for Lövborg, and she has another ready for Brack, should he too prove troublesome.

XL

Then come the two comrades to the Tesman household: Thea and Eilert with their precious understanding. To Hedda the thought of their happiness is unbearable, shared as it is by a man once rejected by her, and by a woman she has treated since girlhood as in every way her inferior. The best in their lives offends her. But they bring with them also an inspiration. Here at last is an outlet for her estopped craving, and a path unoppressed by the spectres of scandal.

So when Eilert arrives in the second act, she contrives that he stay with her, instead of accompanying Tesman and Brack to a " festivity ". " With you, Mrs. Tesman ? " he asks. " And with Mrs Elvsted ", she adds quickly, as if to assure Brack, Tesman, Lövborg and herself, that there shall be no misdemeanour.

Brack and Tesman retiring to an inner room, Hedda and Eilert seat themselves at a table in the foreground. He recites in low tones the romance of their " past ", now stressing sharply its glamour, and now as adroit inarticulate.

She subtly prompts him in the old emotions, until, his poor coquetry alluring him, he reaches the heights she would wish. He leads up to his master-effect by reminding her of her former " cowardice " in threatening him with a pistol and driving him out of the house. So far in the tête-à-tête she had played with him, testing her influence in restraint and encouragement. At the allusion to her " cowardice " she realizes, however, not merely that Lövborg is trying to produce in her a compensating recklessness in order to renew old relations at a more developed stage. That was to be expected of him. But the reminder reveals to her also in a flash that her principal actor may fail her. In her early affair, he had played the hero, the manly seducer. Now, however, he has been reclaimed: the limelight shines on a quiet and passive figure. As the director of a play might suggest to a " star " who is temperamental the action he dare not demand outright, so Hedda appeals subtly and powerfully to the hero subdued within Lövborg:

> " But now I will confide something to you . . . the fact that I dare not shoot you down . . . that was not my most arrant cowardice that evening ".

The effort is more than successful. She must now as quickly restrain, for the actor is far too ambitious.

"Take care! Believe nothing of the sort!"

XLI

Mrs Elvsted arrives. Then are these three seated together at the table. Hedda's arm is about Thea, but she is free as a bird in her joy. "For only think, he says I have inspired him too". She feels herself timid, a captured thrush, and yet in the air of their love she is brave, winging where hawks falter.

"Is she not lovely to look at?" asks Eilert, turning to Hedda. "For she and I—we are two real comrades." Her pure eyes meet Eilert's: a wistful bond.

And then for a moment there is silence. But the deeper harmony is not sustained, for Hedda speaks sharply, alertly. "But now, my dearest Thea, you really must have a glass of cold punch." She refuses. And Eilert too, in respect for his bond. "But seriously I think you ought to for your own sake . . . or rather on account of other people . . . otherwise they might be apt to suspect that—in your heart of hearts—you did not feel quite secure—quite confident of yourself." "People may suspect what they like—for the present" answers Lövborg, hesitating. The attempt wavers. Though only for a moment. "I saw it plainly in Judge Brack's face a moment ago", she continues ; . . . "his contemptuous smile when you dared not go with them into the other room."

Eilert reacts as expected. "Dared not?" he demands. Then a temporary reassurance. "Of course I preferred to stay here with you and Thea." The comrade fights hard to support him. "What could be more natural, Hedda ? "

A reverse. "But the Judge could not

guess that ", she answers lamely. Then prompts once again in her tentative way : " I saw, too, the way he smiled and glanced at Tesman when you dared not accept his invitation to this wretched little supper-party of his."

A strung and responsive actor " Dared not ? Did you say I dared not ? " "*I* don't say so ", answers Hedda, a little afraid of a 'gag' from the comrade. " But that was how Judge Brack understood it."

A verdict of " cowardice " from Brack instead of from Hedda. He appears less perturbed. " I will stay here with you and Thea ". The comrade now rallies, happy. " Yes, Hedda—how can you doubt that ? "

Hedda is failing, loosing ground. But as she falls back, groping for holds— " Firm as a rock. Faithful to your principles now and for ever. Ah, that is how a man should be "—she finds the fulcrum at last to detach their frail bond from its hinges.

"Well now", says she to Thea, "what did I tell you, when you came to us this morning in such a state of *distraction?*"

XLII

Forstyrret! (Distracted!) After the labour of preparation, the patiently set stage, the forms she has so long moulded move suddenly, with that appearance of spontaneity which thrills the creative mind.

Now Lövborg struts the stage. "So that was my comrade's frank confidence in me?" Thea turns wildly to Hedda: the limelight is blinding her. It even becomes necessary to pinch her arm, she tries to prevent Eilert from accompanying Brack. She is spoiling the "star's" great beginning. So Thea protests in vain—and Eilert departs for the "scene" of the festivity.

Hedda now does the best she can with such raw material, impressing upon her that her security with Eilert is now forever lost, reminding her that she is inferior now as in the old days, when Hedda stood above her in class and threatened to burn off her hair. She is " stupid " and a " little blockhead," and after a night of watching, during which Hedda sleeps soundly, looks " mortally tired ", and must go lie down until the return of the hero.

XLIII

But Tesman returns first. Intent on the hero's mise-en-scène—" Had he vine-leaves in his hair ? " demands Hedda. No, Tesman had noticed nothing. He has something much more important to tell her, however,—he has found the " child " of the comrades, lost on the wayside by Eilert. Hedda demands a perusal, which he refuses : but the news that his aunt is dying gives her the opportunity to snatch it away from him.

Brack enters now with a sordid account of the " star ". Eilert has accused the red-haired Diana of stealing his manuscript : the result is a fight with police relief. Opéra comique indeed—and Brack suggests that Hedda shall leave the wings. But her allusion to her pistols is the cue for his exit.

Enter the wild and dishevelled hero. Thea has risen and hastens anxiously towards him :

"Ah, Lovborg ! At last ! "

—but is repulsed by a gesture—

" Yes, at last. And too late . . . I want to say that now our ways must part."

He tells his heroic lie—that he has torn the manuscript into a thousand pieces. Hedda starts at the " gag ", but sees the effect is better, even if it is original and unexpected." Oh God—oh God, Hedda " cries the comrade "—torn his own work to pieces."

Eilert, not to be outdone, steps nearer the footlights :

> " I have torn my own life to pieces. So why should I not tear my lifework too ? "

No longer need Hedda prompt. As if new-created by her these souls rise free to the supreme of tragedy : the thrill of directing them has passed into an exhilaration she can scarcely control. Now shows the ἁμαρτία in Lövborg's soul :

> " And then presently they will sink—deeper and deeper—as I shall, Thea."

—though to Hedda a mark of her making.

The comrade is dazed by the limelight. She can see through the glare that the " child " has perished, that their companionship is ended. And the darkness that spreads before her is at least real. So Lövborg is left with the stage to himself.

XLIV

"She has broken my courage and my power of braving life out", he cries, after the exit of Thea. Hedda subtly prompts—he is a cad for treating his comrade so heartlessly—until Lövborg, as she intends, is convinced that he is utterly worthless. Alert yet detached, she is ready to hint at the course he should follow, though she has little doubt as to what that course will be. For once, however, she is completely mistaken. Eilert now realises that his former security with Thea had been essential to him, that he could not stand alone, that his was a nature irretrievably broken. Nevertheless, the cleft might have remained hidden, had not Hedda revealed it by her destruction of that security. And now there is nothing left for him—why! let him make a fool of Hedda by first winning her admiration, and then deceiving her. So he assumes the pose of an intending suicide in so convincing a manner that Hedda proffers her own pistol and asks him to do it " beautifully ". Then, without the slightest idea of killing himself, he goes immediately back to Mdlle. Diana and, after the usual imbroglio, is accidentally shot in the abdomen.

Hedda might have survived the failure—her first attempt after all. But in her lust for effect she has over-reached herself. The pistol she gave Lövborg was recognized by Brack at the police inquiry, and Hedda is faced by the alternative of slavery to him, or open scandal. The fear of either of these, the shame of Lövborg's Blutwurst finale, and, very importantly, the danger and humiliation of approaching childbirth so intensify her sensations of inferiority that she seeks safety from them in suicide.

XLV

When the hero's sense of inferiority becomes obvious to the spectator, and when his attempts to overcome it are apperceived by the latter under some such term as " immoral " or " irrational ", he appears as a *villain*. Some obvious mark of inferiority—usually an external anomaly or ugliness (for example, the warped physique of Richard III) is frequently added by the dramatist, in order to make the subsequent " villainy " more plausible to the spectator.

Iago affects us so strongly because, whilst his " villainous " action is coherent, and convincing, so far from being *inferior* he is obviously superior in many respects to those around him. Further, his bids for a superior goal did not take place on the familiar low levels of say, an Edmund or a Richard III. How then does he feel inferior, and how does he try to overcome this feeling ?

Bradley has already answered this question in a brilliant manner. Iago knows himself superior in force of personality, in will, in general sophistication to those around him, and yet " somehow for all the stupidity of these open and generous people, they get on better than ' the fellow of some soul '." Especially does he realize his deficiencies before a love which is something more than " a lust of the blood and a permission of the will ". So his sense of being in some way *inferior* becomes sharpest for him at this high level, and his attempts to overcome it are elevated in a like manner, and unified. He becomes, like Hedda Gabler, " an amateur of tragedy in real life . . . getting up his plot at home " (Hazlitt), but with much more thoroughness than she. For her craving for power is continually coming to what one might call a short focus in little acts of insolence and tyranny, attempts to overcome her sense of inferiority through channels less aesthetic than that of her main purpose, but yielding a more immediate satisfaction. There is nothing of this failure, however, in the action of Iago. His inimical tendencies are only allowed expression in the unity of an evolving art-form :

Desdemona : " Am I that name, Iago ? "
Iago : " What name, fair lady ? " (IV, ii).

He will make Desdemona say " whore " !

Iago gives several reasons for his villainy. Cassio has been preferred to him, he suspects Othello of having seduced his wife and Cassio of attempting such a seduction, he " loves " Desdemona and will possess her, etc. Now an unfortunate tag of Coleridge's has explained the significance of these reasons in an all too easy a manner as " the motive-hunting of a motiveless malignity ". The " motiveless malignity " has been successfully disposed of by Bradley. But innumerable critics have seized upon and elaborated the " motive-hunting ". " Nichts ist ein so guter Beweis für die Unechtheit der Motive, die Jago sich einreden will, als der stets Wechsel dieser Motive ", says Wetz.[1]

Schücking and Stoll maintain however, that in the absence of other evidence to the contrary, these reflections are intended as direct information to the audience, and the motives they reveal are real and not fictitious.

On the other hand Iago's conduct, as Bradley points out, in no way corresponds to these motives. What then is the meaning of their appearance in his reflections ?

It seems to me that the answer to the above question is this : Iago knows the danger and futility of satisfying the tendencies revealed in these reflections in a direct manner, and so he has long since learnt to control, elevate and unite them into a purpose, which, whilst yielding his craving for power the highest satisfaction,

[1] " Nothing is so good a proof of the worthlessness of the motives to which Iago endeavours to persuade himself as the continual change in the motives themselves ".

Wetz (A.) *Shakespeare vom Standpunkte der vergleihenden Litteraturgeschichte.* 1890.

is too cunning to bring him into immediate conflict with his environment. It is as if in the past, when he had felt the force of these tendencies in turn, he had said to himself " Take care ! To satisfy any of these means a trivial, temporary satisfaction, and the almost certain consequence of disaster." And now he allows the imprint, as it were, of these tendencies, long since mastered, to remain in his consciousness as a reminder that just as caution was formerly essential in their restraint, so is caution still essential in the development and direction of a purpose that blends and transcends them.

XLVI

Many have tried within recent years to create a hero of such a character that his cravings for power should not only be elevated and unified like those of Iago, but should be directed along a path that did not run counter to reality, and which led to a real, not a fictive goal. Such creations but play the Thersites to an American Achilles — the Frank Cowperwood of Dreiser[1]. The power wealth wields over men is his aim, and, except for a slight Don Juanism, rather adorning him than trammelling, he steps clear of heroic snares. This Achilles takes care of his heel !

XLVII

The so-called *comic* character, *i.e.*, a person laughed *at* and not *with*, might be provisionally defined as one who is apperceived by the spectator as obviously inferior, but who is himself unconscious of his inferiority as such.

The so-called *comic* character, however, has no existence in reality. If he makes

---

[1] Dreiser (Theodore) *The Financier and The Titan*. New York.

use of his obvious inferiority in order to obtain, through the laughter of others, his own ends, he becomes conscious of it as such, and thereby betrays a feeling of inferiority which springs from a deeper source. Precisely insofar as he knows himself " the cause that wit is in other men ", and uses this knowledge for his own ends, is he tragic.

If the so-called *comic* character is unconscious of his inferiority as such, he is no longer comic. There is nothing intrinsically comic in a physical deformity, a trick of speech, or an inability to adapt oneself to circumstances. These things only become comic in a certain apperception of them—and that apperception always reveals a tragic character. A person who laughs at a man because he is fat, or splits his infinitives, or slips on bananaskins, is no Draco of Bergson or Freud, but merely a tragic character unsure of its own superiority.

XLVIII

The importance of apperception has been obvious in the last two sections. Indeed the tragic in the hero's action is often so incommensurate with its effect that the spectator becomes an essential consideration in explaining the latter. The action of Conrad's heroes, for instance, of Lingard or of Razumov.[1] These heroes move discreetly, and with somewhat of awkwardness, because of their delicate armour—irony. This is at once their protection and assertion, against the world that embarrasses them. If we ask : " Why should we be so deeply affected by this slight evidence of the tragic ? " we are forced to conclude that the latter has been somehow altered in its apperception.

We see therefore how important is the latter process in an analysis of tragedy.

[1] Conrad (Joseph) *Under Western Eyes* and *The Rescue*. London, 1923.

And as a kind of bridge to the study of it let me conclude with a few remarks on the tragedy of Antigone.

"An inevitable clash of wills"—"a conflict between public and private rights"—is this the cause of the tragedy? And the latter certainly seems to me to approach nearer than any other to the ideal tragedy—one that should convey the impression of an ineluctable catastrophe. Yet if the gods are omnipotent, human beings are fallible. For, beneath his shield of public rights, Creon wages a personal battle.

> "Better, if needs be, men should cast us out
> Than hear it said, a woman proved his match.
> No woman shall be master while I live."

And Antigone? Certainly Ismene's warning:

> "weak women, think of that
> Not framed by nature to contend with men."

has not been lost on this noble and beautiful nature, though I shall leave any further consideration of it until I have expressed my views on the apperception of tragedy. But as I turn from the hero to the character of the spectator, her attitude, like mine, is one of question: let her then speak for me:

"Who knows if this world's crimes be virtues there?"

XLIX

I have tried to make clear in the course of this essay that the tragic is the expression of a definite character, and that the forces which determine action as tragic must always act through this character. The distinction of the latter is a feeling of inferiority, whose organic and psychic roots are now known. Or, in effect: all those phenomena in life and in art to which the term " tragic " can be applied are best explained as attempts to overcome a feeling of inferiority, which are always directed towards some goal of superiority.

Character can be defined as that part of

us which can offer, at any moment, the best solution to the problem of life. But, free from time, it is to me an evolving art-form, the expression of a self-conscious force, developing itself through trial and error, to a final complete expression. The sublime hypocrisy of the Greeks has given to us as a symbol of the hero the figure of Laokoon. And in the light of my view that symbol still persists—as of an humanity not yet self-conscious in the best sense, but wreathed in self-doubt and despair.

The nature of this self-consciousness? Rays streak its dawn, hinting a golden noon. The Shakespeare of the " Tempest " must have known something of its nature as Hamlet became Prospero, and Ariel and Caliban, at last servants, flitted and sprawled before him.

" This thing of darkness I acknowledge mine " says Prospero, and the Caliban of our time we can view unperturbed, a servant strange to his destiny, and with a pitiful questioning ever on his lips. Ariel, too, can no longer deceive us. Yet to those who shall one day turn in calm from these figures, the sky may well appear clearer, and one in which even its last cloud is fading. As their vision becomes clear and the wistfulness fades from their wisdom.

For Product Safety Concerns and Information please contact our EU representative GPSR@taylorandfrancis.com
Taylor & Francis Verlag GmbH, Kaufingerstraße 24, 80331 München, Germany

www.ingramcontent.com/pod-product-compliance
Lightning Source LLC
Chambersburg PA
CBHW061452300426
44114CB00014B/1954